Budgeting For a Purpose:

A Guide to Better Finances

Jacob Keel

Intro

What Is Budgeting—and Why Do You Need to Do It?

Establishing a budget is the act of deciding how much of your money you're going to spend on one item, how much on another, and so on, before you're actually in the position of spending the money. Sticking to a budget is the act of following through on those decisions. Creating a budget isn't easy, but sticking to any budget is extremely difficult.

The trick is to focus on the word realistic. It doesn't take much research or many difficult decisions to decide that you're going to spend $200 per month on food.

But if you've never spent less than $500 per month on food, you'll blow your budget right out of the water the first week. Instead, before you begin deciding on the numbers in your budget, you'll need to fully assess your current situation, take a hard look at where you can cut back your financial obligations (both large and small), restructure your debt (if necessary), and see whether you can add income.

Only then are you ready to decide realistically where every penny will be spent.

A budget is a tool, and like all tools, the results you get from it will be determined by how you use it. If you make a realistic budget and stick to it, you can watch your life move forward. If you set unrealistic budgetary expectations and don't even bother to follow through with them, don't think your financial problems are over.

Setting Budgetary Goals

Used correctly, a budget doesn't restrict you; it empowers you. You're going to establish a budget because you have financial goals that are not being met. For example, you may want to:

- Be able to pay all your bills from your paycheck—and maybe have a little left over

- Buy your first house

- Save for retirement but can't seem to find any extra money to get started

- Pay off all your credit cards and never get into debt again

- Give more money to your church or to other nonprofits

- Be your own boss

- Take a vacation

- Stop hearing from the hospital about your medical bills

- Buy a new—or at least newer—car

- Stay home with your baby

- Remodel part of your house

- Pay for laser eye surgery

- Finance at least part of your child's college education

- Buy health insurance

- Rebuild your credit

- Find a way to care for your aging parents

- Finally build your dream house

- Take a leave of absence from your job to work in the Peace Corps

- Go back to school and begin a new career

- Buy the downtown coffee shop when the current owners retire

- Get a whole new wardrobe

Are any of these your goals? If so, budgeting will get you there, even if the odds seem impossible right now. Even if you're stuck in a job you don't like, desperately want to go back to school, have to take care of an aging parent, and have $19,000 in credit card debt, you can meet your financial goals—just as others have done before you. With a good budget, a little patience, and a whole lot of determination, you'll eventually get there.

Thank you for downloading this book. It's my firm belief that it will provide you with all the answers to your questions.

Table of Contents

Table of Contents

1. How to Make a Budget to Achieve Your Goals?

If you are having a hard time with debt, then creating a budget can be a real help. However, it's important that you create a budget the right way. Many people make the mistake of sitting down, calculating all their expenses and then trying to reduce them by some arbitrary percentage such as 10% or 20%.

Where you should start

The correct place to start in creating a budget is by defining your short and long-term goals. Your short-terms goals should be the ones you can expect to accomplish in a year or so. For example, if you're having a problem with debt, your best short-term goal might be to get rid of it. The point is to pick a goal you can expect to achieve and that you can keep track of on a monthly basis.

Next, define your long-term goal or goals. This could be to buy a house, send your kids to college or to save for a retirement.

Now that you know

Now that you know what your goals are, you'll know how much you will need to save every month and can start creating a budget that will get you there. For the sake of example, a short term goal would be the need to save $200 a month towards getting out of debt and another $100 for a long-term goal of investing for retirement.

Track all of your spending

Your next step will be to track all of your spending for at least 30 days. You can do this the old-fashioned way with a pencil and a notepad, or if you have a smartphone, there are many expense tracking and budgeting apps available. Two of the most popular are Mint (mint.com), and You Need A Budget. I recommend one of the budgeting apps because it will take much of the work of creating and sticking to a budget off of your shoulders. For example, many of them will automatically divide your spending into the appropriate categories - food, entertainment, transportation, insurance, medical expenses and so forth.

When you can see where your money is going

When you can see where your money is going, next comes the important part. You need to figure next out where you can make the cuts required to get your spending down enough below your income that you will be able to save for your goals. Getting back to our example, if your goals require you that you save $300 a month, you will need to cut your spending to at least $300 below your income.

The low hanging fruit

If you and your family are typical consumers, there is some low hanging fruit or areas where you should be able to cut your spending pretty substantially. First and foremost among these is food. This is an area where with a little effort, you should be able to cut your costs by several hundred dollars a month. You can do this by a combination of shopping smart and by the use of coupons and store specials. Second, you may find that you could easily save another $100 a month by reducing the amount you spend on entertainment. Sitting at home, eating a pizza and watching a rented movie might not be as much fun as dining out and then going to a theater but it's a lot cheaper and will save you money.

2. How to Maintain a Successful Budget Plan

If you are the head of household, you should always be aware of how much your family spends and many times you may find yourself creating a budget on paper, which is the easy part. Sticking to your budget is a definite challenge! It's great to have a budget written down, but until you put it to action, it is only words on paper. You must make a willing effort to follow your planned budget. You can have and maintain a successful budget when you follow these five simple steps to stay on target.

Budget Commitment

Without a commitment to put your budget plan into action, then all you are doing is just writing words on paper that will soon be tossed into the trash. Make it a daily habit of reviewing your expenses and income so there is always an understanding of where your finances stand, which serves as a consistent reminder to stick to your goals.

Lifestyle Changes

Simple changes in your lifestyle can make it a lot easier to stay within your budget. Packing a lunch for work or school can save you to five to seven dollars a day on average. Multiply that by five to six days and that is twenty five to thirty five dollars a week. Multiply that by four weeks and that's $100 to $140 a month! Now you see how quickly it adds up.

Make it a point to prepare yourself on a weekly basis before going to the supermarket. Start by planning your weekly meals and creating a shopping list that will be just what you need to make your meals. Take advantage of days when a store is offering additional in-store savings. When you shop with a list, you are less likely to overspend and stay within your planned and targeted budget.

Keep Your Focus on the End Goal

When you created your budget, you probably had an end goal in mind. Whether that goal was financial freedom, saving for a dream vacation, the purchase of a new home, or simply getting out of living pay check to pay check. Write your initial goal on the top of your monthly budget as a daily reminder and motivator that you are doing all this to reach your end goal.

Think Before You Spend

When you go shopping, venturing into a mall or store filled with the latest gadgets or new clothing trends will remind you of your end goal. Ask yourself: "Is this something that will help or hinder me from reaching my budget's end goal. In other words, is it something I need or want?" Learning to identify the difference between wants and needs is a huge step in accomplishing your end goal.

Pay Cash Not Credit

When you go shopping, keep your credit cards at home. The amount that you pay in interest will rob you of your savings toward your end goal. Credit cards tend to give you a false sense of wealth when used outside of your purpose budget. If you don't have the cash, then it's probably something not worth buying. Remember, your desire is to stay on target with your budget and this will reward you in the long run.

A budget is meant to give you the liberty to accomplish your real desires and keep you free from the chains of debt that hold so many. Your desire to keep a budget is meant to make your life more enjoyable especially when you stay within your guidelines.

Sticking with a budget commitment where you are willing to have lifestyle changes, keeps you thinking before you spend and paying with cash not credit, will have well on your way to establishing and maintaining a successful budget.

3. Budgeting Your Money Takes Discipline

Budgeting your finances can be rather difficult and frustrating at times, especially if you have a weakness with compulsive purchases - such as shopping for those new and exciting hot items you desire. Realizing you need to set up a budget because you are spending too much is one of the first steps in making a financial change for the better. Many individuals do not come to the realization that they need to set up a budget until they are so deep in debt and are hurting financially to stay afloat. Don't worry, if this describes you, I have been there and I have pulled myself out. Do not let this situation catch you off guard; act now and recognize that you need to be budgeting your finances in order to become financially fit.

After you have realized that you need a budget, one of the first and most difficult steps of budgeting is setting it up. By creating a budget and successfully implementing it, you will be able to see some options you have with your money, such as growing your money (investing), savings and identifying cost cutting opportunities within the budget you want to create. Also, from carrying out a successful budget, you will be able to recognize that you are a happier person because much financial stress has been lifted by tracking your money. Most of all, you will be creating new financial discipline that will last your entire life.

When setting up your budget, you need to gather and write down all of your expenses. Write down every monthly bill that you have (i.e., rent, mortgage, car payment, insurance, utilities, etc.), and how much you spend on all of the other areas in your life (i.e., groceries, eating out, and activities). You should also write down how much you save each month in a savings account and for retirement, so you can include them in your budget as expenses.

When you have a list of bills, their amounts, and when they are due - you need to decide how much you will need to set aside for each bill from your income each time you get paid. A little secret that I use is to divide up the amounts of your larger bills based on how many times you get paid each month - for example, let's say your rent was $800 per month, and you get paid twice a month; you would set aside $400 from each paycheck, so you don't get hit by $800 in one paycheck. When you implement this strategy, you will notice that you have more money left over on the paycheck when your rent is due.

The ultimate goal for your budget is to stay just below budget, meaning not to spend more than you bring home (your income). Budgeting and spending money is a task of self-control every day. You will need to have the desire, dedication, determination, and most of all the discipline to become an expert at budgeting your money. Remember, if you are not controlling your money, it is more than likely controlling you and you are only harming your financial future.

There are many ways to track your budgeted finances - for example; you can use spreadsheets on your computer (excel), money programs such as Quicken, plain paper to write down everything, transaction records and apps on a tablet or smart phone. There is no right or wrong way to track your finances as long as it works for you and your situation. However, from my experience and millions of others, the budgeting software available today can save you countless hours of your time in helping you track your finances. Many of the software programs can sync with all of your bank accounts, retirement accounts, mortgages, loans, and credit cards to help track your finances. With some of the programs you are even able to enter your budgeted amounts to help you stay on track of being just below budget.

With the tools available today, some basic guiding principles, and your determination and discipline, you too can have a successful budget that can lead to a more financially free life.

4. How To Make A Budget That Will Help You Get Out Of Debt

It's unfortunate but true that creating and sticking to a budget is about as much fun as having a tooth pulled without the benefit of anesthesia. But like having a tooth pulled, once budgeting becomes a habit, you'll find that you feel better about your finances.

How to get started

Despite what you might read elsewhere, the first thing you need to do to get started creating a budget is to write down some short- and long-term goals. Why would you do this? I'll address the reason for this a bit later.

Second, you need to gather up every one of your financial statements. This would include utility bills, bank statements, savings account statements, information about your investments and, most important, your credit card statements or statements regarding any other form of debt.

Your income and expenses

Next, write down all of your income. This would be both your regular pay, where your taxes are automatically deducted and any other income sources such as money you earn from selling items on eBay or a part-time job. Step four is to list all of your monthly expenses. This would be all those you have during any month - like your mortgage payment or rent, auto insurance, car payments, groceries, entertainment, utilities, auto insurance, retirement- in short, every possible expense.

Fixed and variable

The fifth step is to divide your expenses into the categories of variable and fixed. Your fixed expenses are the ones that remain the same every month such as your mortgage payment or auto loan payment. These are called fixed expenses because they are unlikely to change. On the other hand, variable expenses are those that can be different every month, including things such as groceries, entertainment, gasoline, dining out and gifts. This category is important because this is where you will be making adjustments.

Total them up

You will next need to total up all of your monthly income and monthly expenses. If you have more income than expenses, congratulations. You will have money left over at the end of the month that you can save for retirement or to pay your debts faster. On the other hand, if you learn that you have higher total expenses that income, you will need to make some changes.

Where can you make adjustments?

If you end up in a situation where your expenses exceed your income, there are always areas you can adjust. Some of the more common areas to cut are your grocery bill, your utilities and possibly your entertainment expenses. One idea to keep in mind is that you are aiming to get your expenditures down far enough below your income to have money left over. Achieving this will leave you excess money for savings or for paying some debt.

Why goals?

If you recall, earlier in this chapter I suggested that you first write down some short and long-term goals. There is a simple reason for this. It's just much easier to stick to a budget if you can see that you're making progress towards worthwhile goals. As noted above, a short-term goal could be to get out of debt while a longer-term goal might be to buy a vacation home. The point is to have goals that you can track each month which lets you know you're getting closer to achieving them, as this can help keep you motivated.

5. Important Budget Considerations to Make It Effective

Creating a budget is the best way to take control of your finances. It allows you to manage your limited resources and ensures that they go to the right expenses. This is particularly useful if you are trying to get out of debt. You need to monitor your expenses so you can maximize your debt payments and achieve financial freedom.

However, not everyone knows how to create their budget. It is not as simple as identifying your income and expenses. You need to make sure that the right details are there to make your budget a success. If you are unable to follow your budget, then you will fail in the long run.

Most of the time, the problem lies with expenses. An income is easy to identify. An expense can prove to be a bit trickier because if you fail to include important factors, you may not be able to stick to it. To help you, here are some considerations that you need to look into while preparing your budget.

The reason for budgeting? You need to define why you need to budget in the first place. Is it to pay off your debts? If that is the case, you should make sure you include a debt payment fund. If it is to achieve financial freedom, you need to arrange your budget so it can lead you towards that goal. By identifying your goal, you get the motivation that will make the sacrifices easier to accomplish.

Rank your goals by importance. Most of the time, your budget is created to either help you get out of debt and save for a big purchase. There are times, however, wherein both are needed. Choose which is the priority at the moment. Usually, the debt is the priority but make sure that you allocate some funds to your savings as well. And if you have more than one debt, it is also a good idea to concentrate on one debt. That means paying the minimum on all the debts but putting extra funds on your priority. That will help you get out of that debt faster and thus experience a milestone in your quest for financial freedom.

Include your fun expenses and rank them. One of the mistakes that people make when creating a budget is to take the fun things out of their budget entirely. This is not advisable because that will make it very difficult to follow. Cut yourself some slack and leave room for the fun things in your life. Just ensure that you rank it according to priority and choose the more economical ways to enjoy them. For instance, renting a movie is more economical than going to the cinema.

Let the household decide on the budget. Unless you live alone, your budget should be a collaboration between the whole family. It is important for you to include them because in one way or another, the changes in your spending will affect everyone. Even your children and especially your spouse should know what the budget is. Identify areas that the whole family can save on. For instance, you can all contribute by packing your lunch to work or school. You can even come up with a family project that can help increase your income so you can fit in all of your expenses - even your debt payments.

The bottom line here is to create a budget that you can follow. No matter how great your budget looks on paper, it is nothing if you cannot apply it in real life.

6. Ways You Can Adapt to Save Money

Saving money is a difficult task for most of the people because fund saving needs proper management of all the processes taking place with money. All the entrepreneurs and the trades, businesses require proper money management. Saving cash is mainly concerned with proper money management. If there is no management system in any entrepreneur or any business, then no money can be saved.

Money management:

There are so many things which are included in funds management, some of them are explained below.

Investment:

When we come to the investment, it means that we are spending funds on some tasks, either we will face profit and success, or we will have to face a loss? These two things should be kept in mind whenever you are about to invest money, so invest only that amount of cash which on the loss you can recover.

Budgeting:

Budgeting means to set up or to plan expenditure within the amount in hands. So if you set your budget in limits of money, then you probably can save lots of money.

Taxation:

Taxation is also included in money management, means when you are setting up the money management level, you can't ignore taxes, because you have to give them at any cost. And if you set your goals including taxes then you probably can save a lot of money.

Banking:

Proper banking can also save your money, means while setting your money plans you have to give a look on its banking too, just because if your banking is not proper then you can face lots of money problems.

All the above things cannot be ignored while you set your goals for saving cash, each of them has its importance.

Cash flow in business:

Lots of funds problems are seen in businesses since not every person can run a business successfully. A business needs the talent of money management. Regardless of the way someone runs a business, if the financial plans are poor, they will face losses and hence little to no money can be made. Instead, money will be lost and the business ruined.

Even a small business owner also worries about his money and cash flow problems. The amount of cash coming into a company refers to to profits. How much is going out of the business refers to losses. This cash flow problem can easily be solved by making cash flow charts and giving each step as much importance as it needs. This means that in a business, proper budgeting and money investment programs should be there. Otherwise, companies can face big losses.

Apart from your business, money management systems are also required at home. Partners can make money plans together so that they don't have to face money problems. Everywhere, saving money needs proper money management. Otherwise no money can be saved.

7. Debt-Free Living: Track Your Expenses

Believe it or not, tracking your expenses is one of the simplest yet most imperative factors in having a debt free life. You might be thinking what is the big deal? Logically, if you have no idea how much you have spent each month, you will not know if you have overspent.

Here are the three tips for tracking your expenses:

Create a monthly budget plan

Use an Excel spreadsheet to create different categories for your monthly budget plan. If you don't have Excel, just write it down in a notebook and make it your budget plan notebook.

Next, divide your page into several columns and write down each category at the top of the column. Your categories may include food, mortgage/rent, utilities, entertainment, travel, household products, clothes, transportation, and monthly debt payment if you have any.

Keep track of your spending at the end of the day

It is really important to take the time to record expenses. It may sound like a tedious job at first, but after a while, you'll get used to it and realize how easy it is to see all of your spending in one place. Furthermore, you will immediately find out what items have been costing you more than others. Therefore, you can adjust your expenses, such as cutting down on unnecessary items.

Make sure you to ask for receipts when purchasing. If the receipt is not available, write down the cost and the name of the item and put it in your wallet, so that you won't accidentally throw it away.

Evaluate your budget plan every week

Total your expenses and take a close look at your spending on each item. Ask yourself if each item you've bought was necessary. Can you live without it? If the answer is yes, then you have just helped yourself save some money, which prepares you for debt free living. If you must have it, can you do with a basic plan instead of the premium one, such as a cell phone plan or cable TV subscription?

The purpose of this weekly evaluation is mainly to help keep you on budget or under budget. You might realize that your spending is way over your budget. Don't worry! Take time to go through each item, analyze it and reset your budget. Your budget should be realistic and meet your basic monthly needs.

8. Ways to Make More Money for Yourself Online

#1- eBay Selling

The first way to make money online is to sell items on eBay. eBay is an online auction and shopping website that allows you to sell your household items online for profit or buy a product from the site and then resell them for a greater profit. It is one of the biggest and most popular of this type of website in the world. One good aspect of this site is that a person can sell almost any item and get worldwide attention.

There are some cons associated with this way of earning, though. Such as the fees correlated with the selling a product. Another issue is that sometimes it can take a lot of work for sometimes a less than satisfactory outcome. Along with all of this, it can be quite difficult to determine the right niche for your products to beat the heavy competition involved with whatever it might be. With all of that said, there is still money to be made.

#2- Sell Your Own and Other Services

The next method of earning an online income is either selling someone else's or your services for a price. These services might include you becoming an online tutor for someone seeking information/advice on a certain subject. It could also be your creating a site and selling proofreading services or language translation for other companies. This plan for making money can be very accommodating as well as lucrative for you.

There are of course some cons that come with this as well. Firstly, creating a unique website isn't always easy. Secondly, is getting people to know about your services or getting traffic to your website. Another problem is that you won't be the only person working this angle, and the competition could already be well established.

#3- Paid to Review

Another technique to make money online is to write reviews for products. Now, you can't simply write a review and post it anywhere you would like. For this, you would need to begin a blog and get a following for said blog. Whatever niche you decide on, you then would invite people to advertise their product on the blog for a valued price.

Though this sounds easy, it has its fair share of difficulties. After creating a blog page, you again have to get traffic to your blog. If your blog has no traffic, then no one is going to pay to advertise his or her product with you. You will also have to come up with valuable content, or the traffic that makes their way to your page will not want to return, though this would probably be the least difficult aspect that I have just presented.

#4- Online Teaching

The next form of online income is teaching others what you have learned. You may believe that this is the same thing as tutoring but it is not. I'm referring to teaching how you became successful in whatever it is that you do. If you have yet to accomplish this feat, then you might not be ready for this quite yet.

That brings me to the cons. Obviously, one is that you will need some experience. Another setback might be that even if you have experience, people might not consider your teachings valuable enough for their money. This is also another online procedure that requires you to trade time for dollars.

#5- Affiliate Marketing

The last system on my list for making money online is affiliate marketing. This is the process of earning commission from a company by introducing a potential buyer to it. This is probably the best known and most profitable online industry. You have the option of promoting as many affiliate products as you would like and with just one you can make a full-time income. You can also create your eBook/product that you can sell personally or have it sold for you, which could prove to have huge profit margins.

The cons involved can prove to be quite a struggle at first. Like some of the other schemes, a major issue with this income stream is generating traffic to your site or affiliate product. It is also valuable to create a website which can scare potential traffic away. Along with these, you must have a way to market the niche in which you're promoting, with good keyword placement.

All of these ways are suitable to make money with. You just must decide which suites you the best. Would like to sell items on eBay or sell a service you can provide to others? Do you want to teach or simply just review? Maybe you would like to make some money marketing a product for other to use? Whatever it is, do some research and get to it! The income you could potentially make would help your budget in a big way.

9. Common Traits That Can Help You Stay Debt Free

Debt freedom is only hard because you do not want to apply the skills needed to make it possible. There are only a handful of people who can do this effortlessly.

These are the people who have the right traits that naturally make them more conscious of their finances.

Regardless of how you think you can be debt free, there are common traits that can help you achieve this state in your life. You may be surprised to find out that you already have them. And even if you do not have them, it is only a simple concept of adapting them into your life. There are tools and training programs that you can look into to help you acquire these skills.

First of all, debt-free individuals are very detail oriented and organized. They keep a close eye on every expense that they make. They have an idea how much income they have and more importantly, where it goes to. The latter may be a little harder to track but using a budget will make things easier. The advantage of this trait is you always know if you can afford something - which keeps you from making bad financial choices.

Another trait is being realistic or practical about things. To be debt free, you should always have a firm grasp of reality, especially when deciding what you can or cannot afford. We all want an extravagant life, but the reality is, not everyone will live that life. You need to be practical when it comes to your purchases. For instance, practical people will perceive clothing as a means to cover the body. Being expensive or branded will not be part of their qualifications in buying them.

Being self-reliant is also a trait that helps keep people from acquiring debt. This means they only want to depend on their resources, and they make it a point to live within their means. They dislike borrowing and being in debt to someone else. This prompts them to save as much as they can so they don't have to rely on others to tide them over financial hardships.

Patience is also a trait that they have. They don't get themselves in debt, especially credit card debt because they know how to wait for the right time to make a purchase. They don't mind saving for something before they buy it.

Debt-free people are also self-confident. They do not need to have the latest gadgets and possessions just to be able to say that they are successful. That being said, it also means they are not materialistic. They know that they are successful because of who they are, and that is enough to make them happy.

The last trait that can help you be debt free is your sense of personal responsibility. Having this trait means you know that every decision can affect your future. Not only that, you know that everything that is currently happening to you is a result of your choices. Despite a wide economic crisis, you could have avoided that by simply growing your emergency fund. That is how you become personally responsible for yourself.

10. Starting an Emergency Fund

In the previous chapter, I mentioned the importance of having an emergency fund. Now, I will go over a few quick tips on personal finance basics regarding starting an emergency fund. I'll discuss budgeting, goal setting, and automating your emergency fund.

Budgeting - The first step in starting your emergency fund is to have a well planned budget that not only gives you an idea of where you are financially but lets you know how much money you will be allocating towards your budget. Budgeting is one of the first lessons in personal finance basics, and when you create a good one, you will find areas you can cut back so that you can put it towards your emergency fund or other financial goals.

Goal Setting - All experts who teach personal finance basics and give tips on budgeting, such as how much money should be in an emergency fund, recommend three-six months income. I suggest a three-tiered goal setting system. Set a small quickly achievable goal of $1,000. Because you'll hit it quickly, you'll be pumped and more motivated to reach the larger goals. The next goals are an intermediate goal and finally, your big goal of three to six months of net income.

Automating - An important step in the budget process will be to determine how much money every month will go towards your emergency fund. Let's say you land on a monthly budget of $100 to fuel your emergency fund. As hesitant as I was with online banking, I must admit that with this personal finance basics tidbit it has saved my life. Just imagine going to the bank once a month and asking the teller to transfer $100 from your checking to your savings account. Tedious? Yes! Do you think you might forget once or twice? I would. With automation, I never do. I go online and set up a transfer from my checking to savings account. I set it up to happen on the 1st of every month, but you may prefer to have it every two weeks, on payday. Do whatever works for you.

11. Budgeting Mistakes That Could Cost Your Business Money

Failure to have a written budget - without a written budget or with no budget at all you're setting your business up for failure. Your business loses money when there's no budget in which to use as a guide to running your organization. Failure to have a budget runs the risk of high costs and overspending. Also, without documentation, it's hard to remember what your assumptions and thoughts were when you first put the budget together.

Costs are budgeted too low - entrepreneurs tend to underestimate the business costs in their budgets. This is usually due to not properly tracking expenses on a regular basis. When you don't track the costs in your business, you're not aware of trends that are occurring in your business. Additionally, entrepreneurs often are a little too conservative, instead of expecting the unexpected and adding a little percentage increase to each cost item.

Not managing cash flow - every business has a cash flow, a certain trend in which money flows in, and money flows out, an infusion of major cash, or months when there's very little cash in operations. If you aren't monitoring the cash flow, you're not aware of when to expect cash based on the types of products and services you provide or based on how you are paid throughout the year. When the cash flow is not taken into consideration in the budgeting process, you're apt to overestimate the amount of cash you will receive in a given year.

Ignoring the unexpected - one very common budgeting mistake of many entrepreneurs is not thinking of what can not go as planned, causing a dip in revenue or a surge in costs. It's great to be optimistic in your budget, but you should also factor in those unexpected costs or a surge of new clients and sales that may also incur more costs and revenue as a result of growth. There's also a high tendency to underestimate or not factor in taxes which could set you up for a high tax bill that you didn't anticipate.

Failure to include a part of your yearly planning process - every new project, every goal, and every objective in your business has a money implication. Failure to make budgeting a part of your yearly planning or goals strategy sessions is a sure way to losing money in your business.

Avoiding these common budget mistakes will help you to keep more of the money you make in your business and will also aid in running your business more efficiently!

12. Tips on How to Deal with Debt Problems

'Debt' is a four-letter word of the worst kind. It's no laughing matter, and being in debt has a negative impact on many areas of your life, including your budget. It can be a vicious circle, where you can't seem to make any headway no matter how hard you try. But don't give up hope! The following tips are how to deal with debt problems so you can get out of debt and enjoy financial freedom in regards to your budget.

Know how big your problem is - A lot of people will try to ignore the problem, hoping it will eventually go away. Other people will keep making payments, but won't look at the details of their remaining debt. Neither of these approaches will help you deal with your debt. You need to take a brutally honest look at how much you owe so you know exactly where you stand.

Make a plan - Now that you know the specifics of your debt, it's time to make a plan for paying it off. You can either pay as much as possible towards your smallest balance until it's paid off, and then go on to the next smallest balance on your list. Or, you can work on paying off the one with the highest interest rate first. Both plans have their advantages, but what counts is that you choose one and stick to it.

Get your debt reduced - One of the most important tips on how to deal with debt is to get the amount you owe reduced. Every part of your debt is negotiable to some degree. Call each of your creditors and see if they can reduce your interest rate, lower your balance, or forgive your late fees and other penalties. You have to be the one to ask for these things as the customer service representatives are often trained not to volunteer this information.

Small steps forward - It can seem impossible to get rid of a lot of debt, and the truth is that it can take time and effort. However, it can be quite discouraging to think about the total amount you owe, and how little impact each payment has on that total debt. Keep taking small steps and know that you are making a dent in your debt. This will help you to stay motivated and keep you within your budget.

Following these tips on dealing with debt will put you on the fast track to getting out of debt. Stick with it because being out of debt is a great feeling that is more than worth the effort.

13. Ways to Make More Money and Maximize Your Business Income

You've been working your business for a while and have reached a point where you feel like you have a good handle on things. Although you are making some money, you know that your home based business is capable of producing much more income than it is. If you are ready to kick your work from home business up a notch, here are a few ways you can make more money from home.

Make More Money in Three Ways

Make More Money by Increasing Rates

The easiest way to make more money is to increase what you are charging for your products and services. By this time, you should have a base of regular customers who are happy with what you are providing them. Raising your rates will produce an instant increase in your bottom line.

There are two ways you can go about raising your fees to make more money. You can do it across the board for old and new customers, or you can simply start charging new customers the increased rate. In either case, make sure you communicate with your customers, especially the old ones, about the rate increase to avoid any bad feelings from developing between you and your clients.

Improve Your Marketing Strategy to Attract More Customers

Another simple way of making more money in your business is to increase the number of customers you have. Now is a good time to take a look at your marketing strategy and see where you can make changes that will attract more customers to you. The nice thing about the internet is that there are limitless opportunities to reach new clients.

If you are like most business owners, then you are probably only using maybe 2 or 3 marketing tactics to get your name in front of customers. Try expanding into other realms. Some marketing options include article marketing, banner advertising, forum marketing, social media, guest posting, blog commenting, blogging, email marketing, and starting a newsletter. These are great ways to increase your group of customers and make more money.

Create Additional Streams of Income to Earn Extra Money

It's never a good idea to put all of your eggs in one basket. Unfortunately, that is what many home business owners do. They sell one product or service not realizing that if the demand for that product or service wants then, there goes their business. A great way to protect yourself against having this happen and make more money is to create additional streams of income.

Even if you are in a network marketing opportunity, you can still create additional products to sell that support your business and help you make more money. Information marketing is a big thing these days, and you can do very well selling an eBook which provides people with the information they need to accomplish their goals. Other potential income sources include a membership website, affiliate marketing, or consulting.

Conclusion

As you can see, whether it's owning a business or in your personal life, budgeting is an important aspect of money management. Keeping track of what you spend at home or in your business can have a positive or negative impact on your lifestyle, depending on how you go about it. It is always a good idea to maintain a budget so as to not overspend, which can have negative effects in the long run. Overspending can also lead to more debt and even things such as foreclosure on a house or business failure. As long as the tips I have given in this book are followed, you should have no problem with finances and your financial freedom!

Thank you for purchasing this book. It is my firm belief that it has provided you with all the answers to your questions. Please kindly leave an honest review on Amazon. Thank You.